If

I know

you will

know.

Hello. I am phumudzo mudau. The founder of change publication and author as well. I have a feeling that I can be of help to you. On this book, you'll find what I can call "data" about how I got started not only to writing, but in publishing books for other people and learn how you can write books, too. You need to bare it in your mind that to sell is a skill that most don't have, I got you. "To write is easy all you have to do is to cross out the wrong words" I say. But I have come to understand that to write is simple and to get a publisher is easy, the hardest part is to get your book to people. Who to sell to? Who will buy? That's what I call hell of work not as to where you want to sell. Especially when you don't know anyone in the industry, that feel is lonely. I have been in conversations with many published authors. The sad part of it is that many published authors are not talking about; how they are selling and their struggles. I have come to understand that there are many things one should know before getting into this industry. It doesn't end in writing and publishing, good but it can be. There are more worst things you don't know after publication such as being charged 40 % of your book retail price by bookstores and 10% of your book by marketing agencies. Meaning already you are out of 50% before your book sell. It doesn't end there, they even choose the price for your book. There is no need to fear or to be scared especially now that you know than getting into this industry without knowing. As a writer some things you need to make peace with them. I am no longer surprised since that has been new normalcy in book industry. When looking around locally and globally. It can be seen that most writers are developing their ways of marketing, publishing and selling their books. In most instances some have started their online selling platforms such as blogs, websites and etc. The market is just calling for this kind of creativity. Some are now having Facebook pages just to increase their selling rate. It shouldn't surprise you if looking on how this generation is turning to be, one can see why some companies have started with eBooks and audio books. This brings us to this saying "you better have a way of creating a sell or you won't sell at all" you better have it your way or be out of the game or chase. You may not understand it but without prior concerns in the public everyone is just thinking on better ideas to better the existing market. Obvious if one can say I buy a book based on the cover, as a writer you are to make sure that your book comes out with a great cover to get more buyers. If ever you pay close attention on how this industry works you are to sell more of your books.

But beforehand that is the situation I am writing this book for. To clear

your frustrations so that you adopt
into this industry fully knowing.
Sometimes talking about bad things
doesn't mean there are no good
things out of it. As a matter of fact it
just keep one firm and prepared on
what lies ahead. Just like me when I
learned about this industry I freaked
out, but had to make peace with it. Its
either you sell or try to change the
system that most are well adapted to.
I mean we can't blame bookstores
they are just trying to make cash as
well, you can't blame the big
publication houses. That's what they
do. Their world against yours.

Believe me when I'm saying "you are
        not alone" I have been there. I
        have been lucky as hell making
        writing a hobby not a career. But

then, one must consider that I did suffer through endless rejections of my work for three years struggling to get a publisher, when I was finally able to interest publishers.

That made me to learn that, Real writers write because of their artistic need, above all. It is a great and miraculous calling, and its pursuit deserves all of one's energy and imagination. Without a doubt, there are always struggles along the way, so I thought I'd share a few of my own, which I think are universal.

I am talking about struggles you might face as a writer, but take courage—you're not alone. Just like any writer in the world, you are to spend nights working on your book but that shouldn't shake you.

Who Am I to Give Advice?

I'm far from being an expert or knowing it all on the subject of publishing and selling books, but I ha**ve done it successfully many times** and I'm honest about the process, the emails I receive daily asking for advice can add a word. There are many ways to get your book published and make money selling books, and I'm happy to share what's worked for me. The truth is I was once an unknown writer, been rejected by big publishing houses. I can't guarantee that I've done things the "right way, or I know it all" but I'm enjoying writing books and

I've been making steady money doing so since 2019, my first book did the rest I can assure you. Hopefully when you read my piece of mind, you'll find that resonate and will for you, too. It wasn't easy and whatever in this book will expect you to work towards them. As a publisher my job is to get your book published, but how it sells its in your hands. That requires hell of work, so if not by pushing with me through your book I can literally do nothing.

**Whoever Said Anything About
Publishing I don't know and I
don't need to know, but I'm
saying Get Writing!**

**First attempts first: most people who
worry about how to publish, how
to look for a publisher and sell
their book haven't even written
the book yet.** In fact, I'd say 95%
of the people who email me asking
for help are still stuck in the "I
have a great idea for a book but?"
question. My say is always the
same: write the book before you
worry about anything else, the
bridge is crossed when you get to

it not when you see it. There are an untold number of half-finished manuscripts languishing in desk drawers. Until you've got a book that is well-written (and well-edited), everything else is a moot point.

If you go the traditional publishing route, chances are good that a publisher is going to want to see a complete manuscript before deciding whether or not to publish it. Sure, established authors can just submit proposals, but if you're an unknown, the publisher will probably not pay you much attention without a finished manuscript. At the very least, they're going to want the table of

contents and some sample
chapters.

Having a few chapters done is not
enough. How will you know what
direction your book will
ultimately take? Maybe the first
few chapters will end up being
redundant, or need to be placed in
a different order. And it's very
likely that they won't be your best
work if you haven't seen how they
fit within the larger context of
what you're trying to say. You will
probably want to change the title,
subtitle, description, etc. before
the book is done. So why try to
market something that is
incomplete, not a sure thing, and
going to change?

So, in case I haven't been clear: Stay focused on writing your book. That's the hardest part, and once you've got that done, there will be tons of options open to you. The publishing industry is evolving so quickly that it's becoming easier to publish a book with every year that passes, so there is absolutely no reason to stress out about how to publish a book that you haven't even written yet.

How to think of writing or Know What to Write?

This question is not easy as it may sound. I think everyone has a book inside them as everyone can

write, anyone who is not illiterate
I believe can write. And every
teacher I know has a teaching idea
or perspective that deserves to be
shared with the world. Don't
doubt yourself! Write what's on
your heart. Write what has to be
written. Write the things that you
will lay in bed at night thinking
about if you don't get them out on
the page. Write about what's
bothers you, write about what
wakes you up in the morning.
Don't worry about how it will be
received yet; that part comes
during for the editing process.
Right now? Write. You will cross
that bridge when it comes.

(where you wrote) manuscript

You will need to have your book professionally edited before you submit it to a publisher or try to self-publish it. Remember, you want your very best work to be shown to the world. It's also helpful to have the perspective of an outside party who's not personally invested in your book. Unless you approach publishers who edits manuscripts. It's better to get brutal honesty from your editor than from Amazon reviewers after the book is published. That hurts!

Talking About Publishing?

There are a lot of paths you can take
    to get your book into the hands of
    readers or to those who sells or
    buy books. The only one I would
    NOT recommend is using a
    "scam", which is a company you
    pay huge amount of money to
    publish your book. That's just not
    necessary in 2020. I have been
    there I remember while publishing
    my first book I paid R17 000 for
    publication and had to pay for
    copies still and market my book
    like hell. It was tough and I cant
    really say it was the thing I was
    proud to do, but I had no choice it
    was either to sell or surrender. The
    company promised to sell but that
    was not the case. I remember

making a print out of 20 books
thinking I will just sell them in a
week or so. Thinking that on my
contact list I do have 50 close
people I trusted they will buy.
Only to find out that out of 50, 5
only bought copies. The stress was
how to sell 45 left copies. My close
circle failed to support me I had to
get out of close contact and look
for better way. Although I started
to market my book through social
media I ended up selling more
than 100 copies in two months.
That was great and one of a lesson
I leant which is not to think of
your close circle when publishing
a book. They are to fail to lend you
the support if that happen to be
the case.

One good options to submit your
book to some publishing houses in
hopes of getting published. I will
never gone that route as for now. I
wanted to have complete editorial
control over my books and also
did not want to share royalties
with a publishing company. I
know that trying to get your book
accepted in traditional publishing
can be a lengthy, frustrating
process. You might want to check
out Scholastic, Reach publishers,
Penguin, and other SA publishing
houses,. Although I do have
connections with people at each of
these publishing houses, I cannot
recommend your book to any of
them. I'm sorry!

Be sure to ask lots of questions about the royalty(money) rate you will receive. You will be surprised that out of every copy you sell you are getting zero rand, whereas the publishers are getting huge amount of money from your book loyalties(money). There are some publishers (none that are listed above) that will pay you a very small flat rate for their book and then the company owns the content and never pays out another dime. You'd do far better selling your book as a PDF(Ebook) on than taking a flat rate from a big publishing house. Don't do it! Never and never! You deserve to earn profits from your book every time it sells. That's me talking.

Another path for me was to start my
own publishing company. After 2
years of being under certain
publishers I was not happy about
their decisions and how my book
was selling. Yes! They were
marketing it. But that was not
what I wanted. I had a dream of
writing as many books as I can so
to be in a position of paying huge
amount of money every time I
publish a book was no longer in
my plans. This is what I chose to
do. I started my own business for
both publishing and consulting
services and called it change
publication as a way of helping
the disadvantaged by big
publishing companies. I
established a name, bought a

block of ISBNs, and set up an account with copy2print company (which does Print-On-Demand printing and handles all book distribution.) This was a relatively simple process that gives me full control over my books and cuts out the middle man: only copy2print and either Amazon or PayPal take a cut from my book sales. all under one company that I own personally(Change Pubpication) I mean it is easy for someone interested in writing to like to work with me or use my publication company because they can see my books and work on the internet. Who won't like that?

What About eBooks? Hear me out.

Formatting your book for mobile readers is not optional. Take it as a must! You need to do it, and it's a terrific way to make more money from your books because the delivery cost is so much lower than with print copies. By the end of 2019, I was selling more eBooks than hard copies, and each year since then, the ratio of eBook sales to hard copy sales has increased dramatically.

I use my company (Change Publication) to format my books for Kindle (Mobile) and paperback. Although it is my company I like change publication because I know that the formatting has been correctly completed for every eReader device and there is a lifetime guarantee on their work, so if the formatting requirements change, they'll fix the books. Besides I do the work by myself.

Spreading the word about your book. A must thing!

Most writers (myself included) HATE having to promote and market their books. It is so demanding. However, it's a little known fact outside the publishing world that even if you have a big publishing house behind you, most of the promotion burden still falls on the author. Publishers rely heavily on authors to blog about their books, share them on social media, promote their book tours, etc. It's a simple fact: no one cares about your book more than you, so you'll need to be the one to help spread the word.

I'm assuming as you read this that your book is neither written nor published yet, which is actually good in terms of promotion. That gives you time to build up a platform for yourself and connect with others through a website, blog, Twitter, Facebook, Google+, etc. but the number one thing to remember is this: share high quality content and do it because you enjoy doing so.

If you don't give away good content
  on your website/blog, no one will
  be interested in reading your
  book. Potential readers need to
  know what you're all about and
  how you write in order to be
  assured that the book will be
  valuable to them. Find a way to
  blog that is enjoyable to you: if it's
  not, then you'll feel like your book
  is a burden and you'll get
  frustrated with the fact that no one
  is reading it.

**Where Should you Sell your Books?
Ops! Where I sell.**

90% of my book sales are made
  online, either through takealot,
  exlcusive bookstores or through

Amazon. Libraries and local bookstores also buy my books, but they find me online, reach to me online, and complete the transaction online. They same as those who want my company to publish their book, most we never met. Book stores and supply stores never factor into the equation. They are just now.

There are literally millions of new books being published, and brick and mortar bookstores simply can't stock them all. And in 2020, you really don't NEED a book store to carry your book. Because they have the widest selection of titles and their prices are rock bottom (hardcore), Amazon has

the lion's share of book sales (and
it's increasing every year). Use
that to your advantage. Or stock
printed copies and sell them by
yourself this gives you full
benefits to your books. Unlike
bookstores they will charge you
40% of your book price and
determine the price of your books.
In the end what will you get?
Peanuts only.

You may find that it's worthwhile to
visit book supply stores in your
area to try to get them to stock
your book, but it wasn't worth it
for me. I was told that my local
store orders all its products a year
in advance and I'd have to come
back in 9 months to even make my

pitch. I'm not interested in working within old-school systems like that and didn't pursue it. That was in 2019 though, and perhaps things have changed. They also might be different in your area.

There are a few in-person opportunities that HAVE been fruitful for me. If you do consulting or professional development, that's a great opportunity to promote your books and make sales. Conferences can also serve as networking places and lead to sales. Try pitching to your school district, local libraries and see if they're interested in buying copies, as well. You need to understand the principle of getting to people as a way of making huge sells of your book. That requires you to avail yourself to your target market.

Can you get rich through writing books?

Don't you ever fall into the assumption of getting more money or rich while publishing a book. That Probably never. In fact you are not fit to get into this industry as it requires more from your pocket than it will into your pocket. You pay publication cost and copies cost. Some even pay marketing agencies. One way or another all writers get to be pocked before they pock in. But the great thing about writing educational or self help or spiritual books is that they have a long shelf life, meaning if selling you can get the money you used and more. The hottest novel only makes the South African National bestseller list for a short time and then it's forgotten. But a good education reference book can continue to sell very well for a decade or more. I first published change my life in 2019 and every year it sells more copies than the year before. In fact, this is true of all three of my books: the more people who stumble across website, the more book sales I get.

This works strongly to your advantage.

I haven't done. I still have more to share, but in the meanwhile let this be of great help to you. If you want to see how my writing and publication works. You are free to buy one of my books and see how that will be of help to you. Reading a book genre you want to write about is never wrong. It gives you the insights on how you should outline your book and work towards that. Try that also and see if you won't improve your writing skills. Take time to visit local bookstores or libraries just to have a look on other books similar to your genres.

THE POINT OF SELLING.

Did you know? Most writers HAD failed to sell just 20 copies of their books. You are better to learn it here than to experience it personally. Selling a book isn't always easy – whether your potential buyer is an agent, an editor or readers. There are many strategies to be considered and many routes to try while forging your way to best-selling author. Take it from these writers who have risen to the challenge with full force and now have plenty of advice to share. Although I wanted to hear more about South African authors I must admit that I didn't get any on hold.

Upon selling, you need to know the kind of bookstores you are to direct your book to sell to.

There are Independent
Bookstores and dependent
bookstores.
Independent bookstores don't
have to work exclusively with
distributors, and the
managers of these stores are
often open to negotiating with
independent authors. All you
need to do is contact them
and ask. They may pay you
up front for several copies, or
they make take your books on
consignment, meaning they'll
pay you after the books (or
some of the books) have been
sold. Examples of
independent bookstores in
South Africa are THE BOOK

LOUNGE in Cape Town, BOOKS & BOOKS in Durban, and SKOOBS THEATRE OF BOOKS in Johannesburg. Therefore dependent are more like CAN, Exclusive bookstores, Bargain, and C.U.M bookstores. Their way of selling books is through agencies or distributors. Therefore it is your business to go with the type of the bookstores which will suite your book genre.

Another option can be getting a distributer if you want to make it to the dependent bookstores. In other words thus are the agencies who will do the marketing for your book. Although it won't be free of charge. You have the option to work with certain distribution companies such as Blue Weaver, On The Dot, and Porcupine Press. This has the advantage of getting your books into dependent bookstores like Exclusive Books and CNA, and if you only have one book, it might be worth checking this out. However, if you have a catalogue of several books (just like myself, I now have 16 books), and you factor in the FEES you're required to pay for warehousing, joining fee mostly is R1500 plus 200

copies or so, and listing each
book in the distributor's
catalogue, the CUT the
distributor will take, as well
as the 40% MARKUP* the
bookstores will add to the
price of your book, this could
very well work out being
more expensive than it's
worth for both you and your
customers at the other end of
the line (who will probably be
paying at least DOUBLE for
your book from a bookstore
than if they bought it directly
from you). You can still
choose either not to sell
through bookstores and sell
by yourself. As either do print
out of your books or let
dependent bookstores use

their printing on demand such as megaprint. But royalties will be low. I now use Copy to Print. They are reliable and their services are good to go for.

I can't give you false hope; It's the bookstore's job to sell your book, not market it. Busy bookstores may be approached by authors often, and they are inundated with consignment offers on any given day. You will be expected to fulfil your end of the bargain in the form of marketing. The bookstore wants your book to sell, but don't expect the store to do the legwork for you. Have a solid marketing plan in place, and let the bookstore owner know what it is. It will show them that you take initiative and have confidence that your book will sell.

If you want your book to sell at a specific store, start a mad-lonely ride (putting marketing strategies into action) campaign to make it happen. Have your friends and family who live and/or shop near the store request copies of your book. Have them stagger their requests so your book establishes a consistent sales record. When you approach that store to ask if they'll stock your book, management will be more likely to say, "Yes!" if

they've already sold some
copies of it.

Along the process I have come to
realise and learn from other best-
selling writers of our time. In
compelling this book; this is what
I noticed from those at the top of
the book chain.

"Always put your audience first.
Forge a strong bond with your
readers by delivering more than
they expect, whether that be the
occasional free short story or e-
book, or a personal touch in your
correspondence with them. Build
a relationship through your
newsletter that shows there's a
human being on the other side of
the book. So many people email us
surprised that we take the time to
write back, saying that most

writers ignore them. Hugh Howey is one of the writers who is doing this right with the little things, like putting sand in his **Sand** print books, surprising readers at bookstores and other little things that endear him to readers. Find your own way to thank readers for investing in you and the worlds you create."

#don't fall into South African style of ignoring readers whenever they try to reach out to them. Instead learn to be there to your readers as David said.

"This might seem counterintuitive, but beginners need to learn when **not** to promote. Newbies often adopt a scattergun approach, thinking they need to do something every day (or week) to promote their book. But it's actually better to concentrate your efforts and do a major promotion on each title every three to six months. It also frees up more time for your most important task: learning how to write better…and faster. The latter is a skill anyone can learn, one which makes the best marketing strategies – 99 cent sales, mailing lists, group promotions, ads on reader sites – infinitely more effective."

"This might sound like a sell-out answer to a lot of writers, but having the right book cover is absolutely, unquestionably non-negotiable. You can have the best story in the world and nobody will give it a chance if the cover isn't right. Although no self-respecting writer would put out a bad story, the truth is that you can sell a bad story if the cover is good. 'The right book cover' isn't just professional, clean and eye-catching [even] in thumbnail size. It's also appropriate to the genre and delivers what that reader expects and wants that your book delivers. In the past, we made the

"Writing is about you, but selling books is about the reader. The title, cover and genre will make a huge difference to how the book sells. So if you want to sell books, do your research into the genres that are popular by studying the top Amazon categories and AuthorEarnings.com. Check out the cover designs, titles and sales descriptions, and use those to model success. Assign appropriate categories and keywords when self-publishing, which will help discoverability."

"Learn how to tell a good story and readers will keep coming back to see what new adventure you have in store for them. What does this mean? Hone your writer's voice, find the right pace, keep your writing crisp and create interesting characters. Readers love to love (or hate) characters, and strong personalities can make even small, transitional plot elements within your story interesting. This is as true in real life as it is in the fictional world. Think about regular real-life examples – grabbing coffee at your local Starbucks, a long, dreary day at the office, etc. – where things got a little bit more interesting solely due to real 'character.'"

"Do what you're best at. Don't make
    yourself miserable doing what
    you think you should be doing, do
    what you enjoy doing. Utilize
    your time where it's best spent. If
    you have a talent and passion for
    blogging: Do that. If you enjoy
    Twitter and know the ins and
    outs: Do that. If you are a great
    public speaker and love attending
    writers' conferences: Do that.
    There's no one way to promote a
    book. Know your strengths, utilize
    your time well and remember that
    at the end of the day, the whims of
    fate and word of mouth are more
    powerful than any marketer."

The title, cover and genre will make
    a huge difference to how the book
    sells. So if you want to sell books,
    do your research into the genres

that are popular by studying the top Amazon categories and AuthorEarnings.com. Check out the cover designs, titles and sales descriptions, and use those to model success. Assign appropriate categories and keywords when self-publishing, which will help discoverability."

As the bestselling author of 15 books, I can tell you without hesitation that the hardest part of a writer's job is sitting down to do the work. Books don't just write themselves, after all. You have to invest everything you are into creating an important piece of work. It doesn't end in writing. You find yourself in a position of selling your book. Regardless how good may be your story you are to be rejected. Imagine the pain of spending your whole only for a book that fails to sell.

For years, I dreamed of being a professional writer. I believed I had important things to say that the world needed to hear. But as I look back on what it really takes to become an author, I realize how different the process was from my expectations. People choose to read whatever they want to regardless the great words in a book just as how people choose a book by its cover. They are mostly to leave your book just by the cover if its not attractive to them that is regardless how good your inside may be.

To begin with, you don't just sit down to write a book. That's not how writing works. You write a sentence, then a paragraph, then maybe if you're lucky, an entire chapter. Writing happens in fits and starts, in bits and pieces. It's a process.

The way you get the work done is not complicated. You take one step at a time, then another and another. As I look back on the books I've written, I can see how the way they were made was not as glamorous as I once thought.

Thus lead me to this question: How to really write a book?

As part of this book. I'll teach you the basics steps you need to write a book. I've worked hard to make this easy to digest and super practical, so you can start making progress.

And just a heads up: if you dream of
    authoring a bestselling book like I
    have and you're looking for a
    structured plan to guide you
    through the writing process, I
    have a special opportunity for you
    if you choose my publication
    company.

But first, let's look at the big picture.
    What does it take to write a book?
    It happens in three triggers:

- **Starting point trigger**: You have
  to start writing. This sounds
  obvious, but it may be the most
  overlooked step in the process.
  You write a book by deciding first
  what you're going to write and
  how you're going to write it.
- **Fueling up and self go on trigger:**
  Once you start writing, you will
  face self-doubt and overwhelm
  and a hundred other adversaries.

Planning ahead for those obstacles ensures you won't quit when they come.

- **Wrapping up trigger point:** Nobody cares about the book that you almost wrote. We want to read the one you actually finished, which means no matter what, the thing that makes you a writer is your ability not to start a project, but to complete one.

I know you might have written a book and its failing you or you want to start. Well whether you are the first or not. This tips are to shape your point of view. I hope they help you tackle and finish the book you dream of writing.

Trigger 1: Starting point.

We all have toy start somewhere.
With writing a book, the first
phase is made up of four parts:

1. Consider what the book is about

Good writing is always about what
you know. You can't just write
what you don't even understand.
Try to ask yourself if you were to
buy your book would you? Or
make argument of your book in a
sentence, then stretch that out to a
paragraph, and then to a one-page
outline. After that, write a table of
contents to help guide you as you
write, then break each chapter into
a few sections. Think of your book
in terms of beginning, middle, and
end. Anything more complicated
will get you lost.

2. Daily writing goal

John Grisham began his writing
    career as a lawyer and new dad —
    in other words, he was really
    busy. You can be expecting to
    write a good book if you spend
    days without continue to write it,
    the next touch attempts may be
    moot point. Nonetheless, he got
    up an hour or two early every
    morning and wrote a page a day.
    After a couple of years, he had a
    novel. A page a day is only about
    300 words. You don't need to
    write a lot. You just need to write
    often. Setting a daily goal will give
    you something to aim for. Make it
    small and attainable so that you
    can hit your goal each day and
    start building momentum.

3. An every day time frame.

Consistency makes creativity easier.
You need a daily deadline to do
your work — that's how you'll
finish writing a book. In all my
books I had to write them in a day
or so but in making sure that I
reach what planed for the day.
Feel free to take a day off, but
schedule that ahead of time. Never
let a deadline pass; don't let
yourself off the hook so easily.
Setting a daily deadline and
regular writing time will ensure
that you don't have to think about
when you will write. When it's
time to write, it's time to write.

4. A place to write.

It doesn't matter if it's a desk or a
restaurant or the kitchen table. It
just needs to be different from
where you do other activities.

Make your writing location a special space, so that when you enter it, you're ready to work. It should remind you of your commitment to finish this book. Again, the goal here is to not think and just start writing.

Trigger 2: a time for Do's

Now, it's time to get down to business. Here, we are going to focus on the next three tips to help you get the book done:

5. *Do word counting*

Begin with the end in mind. Once you've started writing, you need a total word count for your book. Think in terms of 10-thousand work increments and break each chapter into roughly equal lengths. Here are some general guiding principles:

- 10,000 words = a pamphlet or business white paper. Read time = 30-60 minutes.
- 20,000 words = short eBook or manifest about 18,000 words. Read time = 1-2 hours.
- 40,000–60,000 words = standard nonfiction book / novella. Read time = three to four hours.
- 60,000–80,000 words = long nonfiction book / standard-length novel.

6. *weekly deadlines*

You need a weekly goal. Make it a word count to keep things objective. Celebrate the progress you've made while still being honest about how much work is left to do. You need to have something to aim for and a way to measure yourself. This is the only

way I ever get any work done:
with a deadline.

7. Never look for feedback.

Nothing stings worse than writing a
book and then having to rewrite it,
because someone look at it and
gave you a negative feedback. It is
better to Have a few trusted
advisers to help you discern
what's worth writing but don't see
them as your go ahead towards
your writing career. These can be
friends, editors, family. Just try to
find someone who will give you
honest feedback early on to make
sure you're headed in the right
direction.

Last Trigger 3: Wrapping up.

How do you know when you're
done? Short answer: you don't.
Not really. So here's what you do

to end this book-writing process
well:

8. Commit to spreading the book.

No matter what, finish the book. Set a
deadline or have one set for you.
Then release it to the world. Send
it to the publisher, release it on
Amazon, do whatever you need to
do to get it in front of people. Just
don't put it in your drawer. The
worst thing would be for you to
quit once this thing is written.
That won't make you do your best
work and it won't allow you to
share your ideas with the world.

9. Accept failure

As you approach the end of this
project, know that this will be
hard and you will most certainly
mess up. Just be okay with failing,
and give yourself grace. That's

what will sustain you — the determination to continue, not your elusive standards of perfection.

10. Moving to second book

Most authors are embarrassed by their first book. I certainly was. But without that first book, you will never learn the lessons you might otherwise miss out on. So, put your work out there, fail early, and try again. This is the only way you get better. You have to practice, which means you have to keep writing.

Every writer started somewhere, and most of them started by squeezing their writing into the cracks of their daily lives. That's how I began, and it may be where you begin, as well. The ones who make

it are the ones who show up day
after day. You can do the same.

Should I tell you, The
reason most people never
finish their books?

According to the book statistics;
Every year, millions of books go
unfinished. Books that could have
helped people, brought beauty or
wisdom into the world. But they
never came to be. And in one way
or another, the reason is always
the same: the author quit.

Maybe you've dealt with this. You
started writing a book but never
completed it. You got stuck and
didn't know how to finish. Or you
completed your manuscript but
didn't know what to do after.
Worse yet, you wrote a book, but
nobody cared about it. Nobody
bought or read it.

#I've been there before.

In fact, the first couple books I wrote
didn't do that well at all — even
with a traditional publisher. It
took me years to learn this, but
here's what nobody ever told me:

**Before you can launch a bestseller,
first you have to write one not
think of one, they say. How do
you write one then?**

What I mean by that is so many
writers sit down to write their
masterpiece, assuming that's all
there is to it. Just sit down and
write. But as I've studied the
world's most gifted and successful
authors, I've noticed this is not
what the masters do. They are far
more intentional than simply
sitting and letting the words flow.

Every great writer needs a system
    they can trust. You and I are no
    different. But an author's system
    for how they produce bestselling
    book after bestselling book is not
    always the easiest thing to access.
    So, as a matter of survival, I've
    had to figure it out for myself and
    created a timeplan that works.
    This is what I call the "The writing
    operating Method" which helps
    me get a book written and ready
    to launch.

This is the part that I never learned in
    any class or school. Producing
    work that sells is not just about
    writing what you think is good.
    It's about finding an idea that will
    both excite you and excite an
    audience. It's about being
    intentional and thinking through
    the whole process while having

proper accountability to keep you going.

In other words, the writing process matters. It matters a lot. You have to not only finish your book but write one worthy of being sold. And if you want to maximize your chances of finishing your book, you need a proven plan.

Writing books has changed my life. It helped me clarify my thinking, find my calling as an author, and has provided endless opportunities to make an impact on the world and a living.

Other things to consider as you write!
There you go.

11. One chapter at a time

Write and publish a novel, one
chapter at a time, using change
publication tool guide.

12. Write a shorter book

The idea of writing a 500-page
masterpiece can be paralyzing.
Instead, write a short book of
poems or stories. Long projects are
daunting. Start small. I have been
publishing books for my clients
around 25 and above pages.

13. Start a blog or YouTube channel or Facebook page.

I remember on my first book I started
a blog, sharing my insights with
people around the world. That

often helps break up the overwhelm. Start a website on WordPress or Tumblr and use it to write your book a chapter or scene at a time. Then eventually publish all the posts in a hardcopy book. This is a little different than tradition blogging, but the same concepts apply. In book industry sharing is marketing and selling at the same time.

14. Keep an inspiration list

You need it in order to keep fresh ideas flowing. Read constantly, and use a system to capture, organize and find the content you've curated.

15. Keep a journal

Then, rewrite the entries in a much more polished book format, but use some photocopies or scans of the journal pages as illustrations in the book. You could even sell "deluxe" editions that come with photocopied versions of the journal.

16. Blog or share consistently

Some days, it's easy to write. Some days, it's incredibly hard. The truth is: inspiration is merely a by-product of your hard work. You can't wait for inspiration. The Muse is really an out-of-work bum who won't move until you do. Show her who's boss and that you mean business.

17. Take frequent breaks

"There is one main reason why we procrastinate: It rewards us with temporary relief from stress." If you're constantly stressed about your unfinished book, you'll end up breaking your schedule. Instead, plan for breaks ahead of time so you stay fresh: minute breaks, hour breaks, or even multiple day breaks.

18. Take care of distractions

Try tools like Bear or Scrivener to let you write in a totally distraction-free environment. That way, email, Facebook, and Twitter won't interrupt your flow.

19. Write where others are writing (or working)

If you're having trouble writing consistently by yourself, write where other people are also working. A coffee shop or library where people are actually working and not just socializing can help. If you're in a place where other people are getting things done, then you'll have no choice but to join them.

20. Don't edit as you go

My English is bad, sayings. Instead, write without judgment first, then go back and edit later. Besides there a bargains of software or editing Apps one may consider such as #spell boy or grammarly. You'll keep a better flow and won't be interrupted by constant criticism of your own work. And you'll have a lot more writing to edit when it's time to do so.

Let me add some of the things I am currently doing as my way of selling books. You will be surprised how easy is that.

- The first thing I did was to Switch to eBook-first marketing plan (switch marketing images to eBooks, talk about the eBooks, make eBooks top-of-mind so more buy those versus physical copies)

- Promote that your paperbacks are on other websites (Takealot, loot, etc.) instead of sending them right to Amazon

- Have any collaborators or those who sell your book via an affiliate link with Amazon switch to a different distributor or an eBook link for the time being

- Reduce your eBook price or run a special to get the word out

- Connect the current events to your story or message (it's a GREAT time for dystopian authors and those with work-from-home material)

- Offer a free PDF for anyone who
  buys a paperback (so they can
  start reading right away, waiting
  until their physical copy arrives)

- Run a special discounts offer to
  your readers.

- Make sure that while still
  promoting, you're aware of others'
  struggles and hardships during
  this time. Be sensitive with your
  messaging. Understand when
  someone is saying he is broke, or
  wait till month end.

I know that marketing is hard and
whole of a work. But it is the best
way of selling your books. In other
words its more like saying "you
don't know my books so I am
making them known to you" once
people know about them they are
to buy and share about them. This

requires a great relationship with your target market. As a way of gaining their full support. Theirs is no need to brag about it. The reality I have come to know is that every writer is making ways of selling better and that comes with a marketing strategies. Obvious I know more since I'm a publisher. When people approaches me they ask questions like that.

"If you want to know why it is important to market your book, the profits will show you that". Your book is just a book and for it to sell that needs you not your publisher.

Let me show you my marketing means. If you follow me on my

digital platforms you already have an idea.

Some of the tips before getting to what works for me. Marketing a book on social media: build a fun base. For instance; Facebook- to succeed most created a page for themselves or about their books. Posting book content or video. Posting blog posts. #Blog through posting and creating mail list. #Twitter and Instagram using #tags, post catching tweets. Posting pictures related to their book. Yes! I even use WhatsApp in most instances to market my books. Since my fun base is on my contact list.

To sum thus up. It is clear that all
platform requires you to do the
following.

Publish your book's landing page on
your site.
– Post blogs about your upcoming
book
– Create a countdown timer for
the book's release date.
– Set up an affiliate link to your
Amazon page so you get
commissions on book sales
Include sample chapters from
your book
– Link to video clips about the
book on your website
– Communicate directly with your
email subscribers about new
releases or your current blog post

It is an easy task to do the marketing
if you have the right tools. It is
also clear that such media
platforms can be of great helping

in shaping the success of your
book.

To market your book it doesn't end
in social media platforms. That is
the beginning of marketing. The
most aspects of all is to get
influencers to market your book. I
mean do you really think your 15
viewers on WhatsApp and 5 likes
on Facebook will help you selling
your book? I mean as a new kid on
the block it doesn't surprise me
that you might not be popular.
Most are gifted since they are
popular and liked by many. But
those who are not popular on
those platforms also can sell their
books through influencers. Look
how other big brands sell their
products. Through emails, radio
show and TV show. You can't
afford that, why not choosing an
influencer suitable for your book?

Influencers can be podcasters,
	bloggers, or authors with strong
	email lists. It's someone with an
	established platform that can get
	you noticed if they notice you.

An influencer is someone who has a
	lot of promotional weight and can
	spread the word about your book
	to thousands of people with just a
	brief mention to their email list, on
	their blog, or by sharing on social
	media, for example. Don't you
	think your book needs that? I
	mean to have someone to spread
	the word out for you. In doing so
	one should always look at the
	bigger picture. Many likes won't
	sell your book. This simply means
	that a suitable influencer must be
	someone interested in reading
	books. Someone who's close circle

are book readers. You can't pay an influencer who will just get you likes and zero sell. That will be a waste of money and time.

But still take a note: There's plenty of self
described influencers people who say, "I'll promote your book to my 200K followers." Don't take the bribe! You are better off spending a few Rands getting your messages out to a few dozen people who might actually buy your book than thousands who won't. A targeted audience is the best audience. In the case of buying followers, you might even get banned. While it might sound impressive to

say you have 15K followers, it will come back to haunt you. The only way to start or create fun base is organically; which is going real, through a reliable system you can trust.

You need to bear in mind that social media is a powerful way to promote your book to potential readers. You can get in contact with thousands of people just by hitting a few buttons.

But with social media sites, the big scare is the amount of time you can get sucked into trying to do everything. If you try to connect with everyone, you'll match up with nobody.

When promoting and marketing your book, you can't be

everywhere doing all things at once. You need to make your pick.

That is why **I suggest you choose two social media sites to work with** and post your content regularly on these two sites. This won't confuse your fans. You can't be in all social platforms or channel while selling one thing. That may look like a desperate call or a financial need. To make your book token about in its absence generate selling. Imagine if one post about it on twitter everyone interested will be forced to google it and share to other also. Such also gives your book chance to adapt and be noticed.

<u>**How do you choose one platform then? If I can ask.**</u>

Well that shouldn't bother you. Since you now know your target people. The people you want to sell to then it will be easier for you to pick two platforms out of many.

Lets say your book is about businesses. What should come to your mind is who are the business people? And where can you find them? **Because your book is more business-focused, you may find that LinkedIn works best for you, since it allows you to connect with new readers on a more professional platform.**

You see that's it. You then check if your book for example is more focused on romance and relationships. Obviously aged for youth, Facebook is the best place for that since it consist of many youth dealing with such talks. However, you must put it in your senses that marketing your book in a platform that doesn't suite results in it failing to sell. Even if it's in the right platforms know that the competition is tough, that require you to come up with better offer than the one in the market. Competing with the current and known author will results in a more personal way. That is not healthy.

Let me wrap up this book. By sharing with you about a certain author. Who happened to show off how he ended up selling more than 18000 copies of his book. Using

some of the things been writing this book about. This guy will make you see how you can apply this book in selling your book.

I quote "Two years ago, I published my first science fiction novel, *Where the Hell is Tesla?*, and sold 10,000 copies in the first twelve months. (It has since gone on to sell over 18,000 copies). My second has sold nearly 5,000 copies, and my new release, *Don't Touch the Blue Stuff!* is opening strong, too. So how the heck did all this happen? Was it luck? Because if it wasn't, how on earth did that many people find out about it and buy it? Did I know something — or someone — special that could influence the outcome?

Nope. It wasn't luck. And it wasn't influence. I mean, a few unexpected things turned in my favor for sure, but I strongly believe that if you've got a good book inside you, and you do your homework, and you put that learning to work, that you can sell thousands of copies.

Here are five things I learned how to do on the road to my first 10,000 copies:

1. WRITE YOUR BEST BOOK

It sounds obvious, I know. But there's an entire world of badly-written, poorly-edited self-published work out there. Because the tools have become so easy to use, there's a temptation to get *anything* out there, without going through the rigors of research and editing, in hopes of quick discovery and viral success. Don't give in to that temptation. I spent over a year writing my first novel, and almost a year writing my second. If you don't know someone who can competently edit your writing, hire someone. End readers will know the difference. Here's a small example: I released the first two parts of my novel *Where the Hell is Tesla?* as serial stories, like Hugh Howey originally did with the *Wool* series. And though the feedback I got was largely positive, I got ripped for little editing errors. So I learned a huge lesson before selling even one copy of the full novel – the product has to be bulletproof. Editing, spell-checking, formatting, consistency, characters' motivations, plot holes, everything. I don't think all the **marketing** in the world will help a product that's not ready to launch.

2. BUILD YOUR "PLATFORM"

Book marketing consultant defines your platform as whatever plan and methods you use to connect with readers and sell books. In my case, considering the nature of my full-time job, I couldn't consider touring, and frankly didn't have the patience to find a publicist that would actually respond to me as a first-time author, so I chose the online-only path: website, social media, Amazon author pages, and an email list.

- **Website:** Yes, it's common sense, but if you're going to self-publish a book, you need a website to spread the word and keep the conversation going. It's a place for fans to contact you and a way to build your email list. (Here's a **great article** on making the website process as painless as possible.) I actually create content for two websites: **Goldfinch Publishing** and **RobDircks.com**. You'll start with zero traffic, as I did, but after a while (be patient!), if you've got some engaging content and good keywords, you'll see the clicks and the email signups start to come in.

Here are just a couple — of too many to list — author websites I particularly like: **Takalani M** and **Joel Z** These guys are truly great at connecting with their fans.

• **Social media:** I've heard many people advise this and I'll tell you the same thing: don't overdo it. With a full-time job and writing and publishing on the side, this book promotion thing at times tests my productivity limits. So, I stick with

just Facebook and Twitter, and I'd say go with the one or two that feel right for you. For example, if you're creating a graphic novel — very visual — maybe Facebook and Pinterest would be your thing. Journalist writing non-fiction? Twitter. Try them all out and see what feels right for you.

One stand-out example for me is John Scalzi. He's a very successful sci-fi writer with a huge Twitter following. He uses Twitter as a sort-of ever-present sounding board, every single day, many times a day, showcasing his way sense of humour and insistence on being himself. It's awesome.

- **Email list:** Okay, this one is an uphill battle, but worth the effort. As a new author, getting people interested enough to take the ride with you through emails is tough. But since I've started blogging, posting, tweeting and emailing, and my list is slowly growing. I use **Mail** to manage the email list and campaigns. It's an excellent tool at an excellent price: free.

3. RELENTLESSLY PURSUE **BOOK REVIEWS** AND EXPOSURE

I think the single biggest thing that helped sell all those books, beyond the quality of the work itself, was reviews. And here's what I did to get them:

- Prior to launch, I contacted 75 people who agreed to be advanced reviewers, keeping in touch with them over the next several weeks, ultimately launching with 25 reviews on my Amazon sales page on day one. Enough reviews will trigger Amazon to begin recommending it to others. Your book also gains quite a bit of credibility in readers' minds when they see more than a handful of thoughtful reviews.

- At the end of the eBook, paperback, and audiobook, I have a prominent, clear call to action asking specifically for a review on Amazon or Audible, noting that it's the best way for independent authors and authors with small publishers to gain exposure and help sales. More people than you'd think have told me that my simply asking them to leave a review led them to write their

very first review ever. Ask clearly.
Readers like to help!

• I looked up reviewers on Amazon,
Goodreads and Audible on an
ongoing basis, and actively
reached out to these individuals to
provide a review in exchange for a
complimentary copy of the book.
Many people took me up on this
offer. This is tough, tedious work,
but well worth the effort.

• I've also run free giveaways of
book copies, and engaged
members of Goodreads for free
copies in exchange for honest
reviews.

Regarding exposure: I could write a
full article just on this topic, but in
brief, spend time networking with
whoever you can, and investigate
genre websites, and reach out as
much as possible to offer guest

postings, interviews, book
reviews, or whatever you think
that site might find interesting, or
live readings at physical locations
like libraries. To date, for my first
novel, I've probably landed ten of
these opportunities, which isn't a
lot, but has certainly helped me
sell books.

4. PROMOTE YOUR BOOK

- **Email promotions:** Coinciding
  with these Countdown Deals, I ran
  paid eBook promotions through
  book promotion sites that list
  discount deals, and send out daily
  emails to their subscribers. (Some
  post to social media as well.) They
  included BookGorilla, FussyLibrar
  ian, BargainBooksy, Booksends, Er
  eader News Today, and several
  others.

- **Online advertising:** All the major online services offer paid advertising. At one point or another during these countdown promotions, I've tried all of them. Overall? I'd say if you've got the stomach to spend money that isn't returning as high a value as the email blast promotions listed above, but want to boost your exposure temporarily, then go for it. For each of these, you can set a daily budget not to exceed, a start and end date, and live monitoring of response. I set my daily budgets at between R50 and R20 per day for a week. I've run Facebook/Instagram ads, Google ads, Amazon ads, Twitter ads, and more. (I'm constantly experimenting, with varying degrees of success).

- **Social Media:** As a matter of course, during each of these promotions, I got the word out as much as possible through Facebook and Twitter.

The result? The four promotion periods, unsurprisingly, showed the largest spikes in sales".

Well, well. I can only say the selling of your book is in your hands. If you start to practically do what you have read about in this book you are to sell. Up today my books are still selling that is why you even have a copy, it is a clear proof.

<u>Should you be thinking of making writing a career?</u>

Well I have something to say regarding the above question. Whether writing as a career or hobby we all have one thing in common to think about "money". Very few writers actually make a living at their writings. If you are a writer yourself, you know this already. People will tell you to give it up and get a real job. This is why most writers write only on the side or totally give up the writing thing after awhile. It can be quite frustrating. The toughest thing to do is to remain positive while facing adversity. It wasn't easy for me and don't expect it to be easy to you as it was not to everyone.

Many successful writers did exactly that. They kept writing even though it seemed like it was hopeless. Friends and family would often tell them to give it up, and focus on other aspects of their lives. But when you are the person chasing your dream, giving up is often not an option. If you are a true writer, then you realize that writing is something that is in your soul. To give it up would be impossible. But one can ask "how do you get the money to publish your book if you are not working?" I mean the publication costs and one can't be writing without getting his books published. When trying to look for sponsor it isn't an easy thing to do. Obviously you now can see that in order to get around the clock whether writing as a career or hobby one should have something to pop up in making their writing dream come true.

Let's look at some very successful writers who did not start out that way. It turns out he wasn't a doctor at all! However, he is one of the most successful writers of all time. His books have sold over 600 million copies.

His original goal was to become an English teacher. But his future wife convinced him to give up wanting to become an English teacher, and convinced him to pursue drawing instead. They later married, but he never did have any children of his own. He originally drew political cartoons for papers and magazines. Eventually he turned his attention to children's books where he did both the writing and illustrations.

His first children's book. It did not
     start off a smashing success
     though. He sent it around to
     numerous publishers and they all
     turned it down. In fact, it was the
     28th publisher he sent it to that
     decided to take a chance on it.
     Vanguard Press ended up selling 6
     million copies of the book. It's a
     good thing he did not give up
     after the 27th publisher rejected it.
     It just goes to show you that good
     fortune could be just around the
     corner. But first you have to turn
     that corner before you can find it.

Although, he made it doesn't mean
     everyone can. You must just
     prepare yourself for anything.
     Even after being rejected you must
     always hold on to your dream
     until it come to pass. You have to
     understand that what I have been
     writing about won't do the work

for you. You still have to work on it and make it work for you. You are fortunate to come to learn about things some experienced. Something that makes whoever come in contact with powerful. I mean to know is better than not to know in this industry.

Most people refuse to share what they know not because they don't know, but because they want to remain on top and those below. I mean most people are selling their books very well and some are not. It simply shows that some knows the better way of selling than others but not sharing. I mean a business line shouldn't be a secret. This kind of thinking has resulted in most books that would have been great to be undermined. Regardless how good the author at the bottom can be he won't be

recognised by those on top. It is
not a bad thing, it is just a way of
saying "find your way to the top
by yourself" that results in
creativity and a selfish way of not
willing to uplift the upcoming
writers. Once one finds his way to
the top he pass the same story to
those at the bottom "find your
way to the top". The only thing
they share is that which they are
benefiting from. Obvious if you
are a distributer you share how it
works because in doing so you get
cash. But if not it is a bite by bite.

<u>*Allow me to go into details how I applied what I was writing about from page one of this book*</u>

How did I managed to sell more than 100 copies of my first book #change my life in two months after failing to sell 20 copies in three months: starting my writing career, writing a book was difficult. It could take hours, days, weeks, months, and years of hard work. I can still remember it very well as in writing my first book it took me 4 to 5 years, just to get done with 179 pages. As from changing words and pages was another reasons. But after these years I can tell that writing a book is easy as pie compared to actually selling your book. Besides, you have Novelize to help you write your book. But how do you sell your first 20 to 100 copies after you're ready to publish?

Although I built a blog and had a great marketing plans that I learnt from other writers and online as well. There are lots of different strategies for selling books. Many successful authors claim that they were able to sell lots of books by building a solid platforms for selling on. Just like myself I thought I had a perfect plan to sell my book, thinking of reaching out to my friends, family and church members. Although they supported a bit but that couldn't help me to sell 20 copies. I think It only helped me to sell 15 or so copies. I was so frustrated not knowing how was going to sell 5 copies left with. I tried to send text messages to people I know, some responded, some they didn't. I then went on sending WhatsApp texts and posting that really helped me in selling 5 copies was left with. But that was in a period of three months.

How did I sold 100 copies in a period of 1 to 3 months. Firstly I launched a book promotion campaign, running it through those who purchased copy of my book. Just to ask them to offer reviews about my book on any media platforms and post a picture holding my book. That I called "spreading the word" within a month I got calls from people saying their friends needs a

copy as well. The relationship was
built and it was running well. I
even approached churches
wherever I went to visit churches
to pitch about my book since it
was related to God, that's target
market. It helped as pastors of the
churches I went to encouraged
church members to buy a copy.
Sometimes I would gather emails
of pastors in making mail list to
pitch my book to them. That made
my book to be in demand and
pastors words made a great selling
breakthrough for my book. After
going to churches I went on
visiting libraries and local
bookstores to pitch my book. The
book went viral, sometimes I
would receive calls from the
people I didn't know wanting a
copy. The last platform I went on

using was reaching to national newspaper. Just to appear on the news side made a huge difference. Thus reminded me that every writer need to publish early and often. Whether you publish your book in excerpts on your blog or another platform doesn't really matter. If the story is good, people are going to want to know what happens next. That means they'll come back to read your next chapter.

Of course, you may have already finished your book, so it's a little late to follow this advice. Don't worry. There's still hope for you as you are now learning from this book.

Good writing sells. Upon receiving
calls and mails what made people
to be interested was what was in
there for them. Obvious before
one may think of buying a book
what they may ask themselves is
this question "what is in this book
for me? Will it be something my
life needs?" If it does such person
will end up buying it. Most callers
would say " I love what people are
posting about regarding your
book" I have a friend who I think
should read it. Throughout the
process I learned that one person
may love your style, and the next
person may hate it. But if you
want to sell books, your writing
should be good. That goes without
saying. How will you know
whether your writing is good
enough?

The easiest (but not cheapest) thing you can do is hire an editor to proofread your work. You could also try to find some beta readers. Beta readers can help you determine whether your book is fun to read, but they probably won't pick up on all of your spelling and grammar errors. Of course, you should also spend some time on editing the book yourself before you send it to a beta reader or editor.

Another thing upon selling. You need to know that Customers just don't like buying books that haven't received any reviews. Having a lot of reviews won't guarantee that you sell a lot of books, but it'll surely increase your odds. The algorithm for book

rankings is complicated. It
includes number of books sold as
well as number of positive book
reviews. You obviously need both,
but it helps to start somewhere.
Just two good reviews can take
your book somewhere. Avoid
getting reviews from relatives. Get
an honest reviews from people
who bought your copy, people
you are not related to. Obvious if
you see someone we share the
same surname on my book
reviews that won't probably make
difference. You need to know that
reviews are not given freely. You
must earn reviews for what your
book is about. Just make sure you
ask reviews to the right people.
Someone who reviews Fantasy
books won't be interested in your

romance novel, so don't bother
them.

As a new writer there is no need to
be in hurry for your book to sell.
Some books can take years before
selling depending on the plan and
goals you are setting for your
book. Another thing which I did
and it helped me was giving away
free copies of my first book for
reviews. The response was not as I
expected. Out of two people that I
gave a free copy non of them
bothered to replied. I was so down
but in the process of writing their
reviews were positive. But still I
advice you to give away free
copies as that did helped me in my
second books. There are lots of
fiction writers. But there are not as
many fiction writers who have

published a lot of books. One of the best ways to get faithful readers is to keep writing books. And in order to attract a new reader, you may want to consider giving one of your books away for free. For example, it might be a good idea to give away the first book of your trilogy. If it's well written, your customers will buy the second and third book. But this strategy could also work well with other stand-alone books.

The great thing about giving books away for free is that your free readers still help you increase your rankings in the online bookstore. You may also get a review or two out of it. But most importantly, it's a risk-free way

for readers to see that your books
are worth their time.

This book has some good ideas for
marketing your book, but not all
of them will work for everyone.
That's why it's important to
measure what works. If listing
your book for free decreases your
sales and doesn't boost your rank
significantly, then maybe that's
not a good option for you. If your
beta readers are excited about
buying a paperback book from
you, then you don't need to talk
them into accepting a free eBook.
If you only want to write one book
and have no desire to establish a
huge readership, then maybe you
don't want to do anything to
market your book. There is always
something in for you. Knowing

and understanding who your
target market are will make you to
make a perfect selling plan that
will work. You won't find yourself
in a position of forcing someone to
buy your book just because they
know you. That is not how it
works, let people buy your book
because its good and they like it
not because they know you. Those
who buyers your book and end up
not reading it won't be of help in
you selling your book. But if they
buy your book and you take time
to ask for their reviews that will
obviously create sell. Still if they
can't assist you with that let them
be. Just because you are now a
writer. It doesn't mean everyone
should become a book lover or
buy your book. Perhaps it might
have happened to you before you

start writing, not a friend of books and never buy other people books. Did they forced you to buy their books? Now that you are, sometimes posting about another author upcoming book won't hurt but that can work for you in return. You should know that it is not every writer that you post their work that will post yours. You should do it because you like their book or you want to not because you expect them to do the same. I have been in contact with writers who posted my books not because they liked them but because they wanted my attention. What makes a writer to listen is when another writer is in support of his books through buying them. To understand the feeling and position of another writer can sell your book. Since your personality can contribute for your book to sell especially by those who knows you. My mother once said to me, "son make sure that you write about what your life is. People should buy your book and see your life in it not just a mere writing" for example if your book is about kindness and you are not kind towards people, it is obvious they won't be interested in buying your book.

Mind you I was once a writer, and I am now a publisher. I work with a lot of writers, and by far the most frustrated, disappointed, and confused writers I work with aren't the ones chasing after the publication of their first book,

trying to figure out how to publish
a book for the first time. Not even
having funds to publish their
books with me. It is the ones who
have already published their first
book.

You probably don't think this could
happen to you, do you? But I've
talked with enough first time
authors suffering from the same
frustrated that I know this story is
closer to the rule than the
exception.

It doesn't have to be like this. But to
avoid this experience and discover
how to publish a book
successfully, it's not enough to just
do more — more promotion,
spend more money.

You have to completely change your approach to publishing and follow what I have been trying to explain in this book. I can tell you that, Frustrated authors expect readers to flock to their writing as soon as it's published. But Successful authors realize they can't do it alone. They share their writing generously, early, and often, and they build connections with other writers and readers who will be excited to share.

The best part of all these principles is that they work regardless of whether your books are self-published or traditionally published. No matter how you choose to publish your books, you can magnify your reach (and sell more books!) using the steps above, just as from page one of this book.

So go and share your writing. Share early, share often, and share generously. And do what you read about in this book. I can't wait to receive an email or text from you saying how this boom helped you to sell. I am writing because I care and want to see your book selling. Your selling story is going to change. With no doubts this book is behind all the way to your selling success and long lasting writing career. It is only the beginning. Cheers!